My Body Is My Own

Learning Consent, Respect, and Responsibility

Words by Tracy L. Hawkins
Illustrations by Lola Svetlova

DEDICATION

For Kevin, Rowan, Alder, and You

As a baby…

I can tell someone when I am hungry or tired.

I can grow bigger and stronger.

I can discover what brings me comfort.

My body is my own.

As a toddler…

I can help brush my teeth and wash my hands.

I can stay with my grown-ups while crossing the street.

I can let people know when I don't want a hug.

My body is my own.

As a preschooler...

I can visit the doctor and the dentist.

I can wear a coat when it's cold outside.

I can ask before I touch someone and use gentle touches when I do.

My body is my own.

As a kid…

I can eat a variety of foods so that my body has the nutrients it needs.

I can drink plenty of water.

I can wash my body to keep it clean.

My body is my own.

As a big kid...

I can be proud of my body and its abilities.

I can express my boundaries.

I can respect the boundaries of others.

My body is my own.

As a teenager…

I can make healthy decisions about touching other's bodies or letting others touch my body.

I can make safe choices while driving.

I can participate in activities that make me happy.

My body is my own.

As a young adult…

I can get enough sleep.

I can follow my hunger cues, not eating too much or too little.

I can express my emotions and ask for help if I need it.

My body is my own.

As an adult…

I can move my body to keep it strong and healthy.

I can reduce the stress in my body.

I can care for others.

My body is my own.

As an older adult…

I can be purposeful about how and when I move my body.

I can take responsibility for going to the doctor when I'm sick.

I can think and say positive things about my body.

My body is my own.

ABOUT THE AUTHOR

 Tracy L. Hawkins is an Associate Professor at the University of Wisconsin-Whitewater, where she teaches sexual ethics. She is also a mom to two preschoolers.

ABOUT THE ILLUSTRATOR

 Lola Svetlova is an artist and illustrator based in Russia, Siberia. Her main focus is children's books.

Please check out our second book: "My Body Tells Me How I Feel"

Made in the USA
Middletown, DE
26 October 2021